SEASONS OF WINTER

CHRIS TUTTON

AVALANCHE BOOKS

Published in Great Britain by Avalanche Books, England.

Copyright © Chris Tutton 2005.

The author asserts the moral right to be identified as the author of this work.

British Library Cataloguing in Publication Data. A catalogue record for this book is available from the British Library.

Printed in Great Britain by SRP, England.

ISBN 1 874392 23 4

All rights reserved. No part of this publication may be reproduced, stored in a retrieval system, or transmitted, in any form, or by any means, electronic, mechanical, photocopying, recording or otherwise, without the prior permission of the publishers.

This book is sold subject to the condition that it shall not, by way of trade or otherwise, be lent, re-sold, hired out or otherwise circulated without the publisher's prior consent in
any form of binding or cover other than that in which it is published and without a similar condition including this condition being imposed on the subsequent purchaser.

For dear Roo, with love.

Contents

A Complex Absolution – The Protracted
   Geometry of Forgiveness   9
The Fallow Yield   10
Reporting for Duty   13
Vista   14
April Sarabande   15
The Count   16
The Long Day Has Fallen   17
A Lingering Eclipse   18
The Betrothal   19
A Continued Point of Arrival   20
Old Age is a Bloodthirsty Bastard   21
Philosophical Musings. The Male Fantasy
   Dignified, and the Negative Influence of
   Logical Positivism on the Already Putative
   Reality of Romantic Love   22
Condition of Existence   23
Childhood   24
In Praise of Despair   25
Remembrance   26
Symphony   27
The Search for Beauty is the Seed of Prayer   28
Narcophobia #2 – Shipwrecked in Limbo   29

Beachcombers	*30*
Questions for all Ages	*31*
The Great Starting Gun Crime – Another Senseless Statistic	*32*
Harbour Days	*33*
Seasons of Winter	*34*
An Unexpected Opportunity Presents in the Unquiet Pitfalls of Reason	*35*
A Ruby Anniversary of the Star-crossed, Cold Cast, Snake-eyed Marriage of Blood and Ash	*36*
Another One of Those Awkward Moments	*37*
A Good Education Wasted on the Pursuit of Knowledge	*38*
Lightning Strikes the Same Place Twice to Save the Stricken from Moving	*39*
The Courtship Ritual	*40*
The Question	*41*
A Simple Transmutation	*42*
A Resilient Opponent	*43*
A Permanent State of the Temporary	*44*
Massacre	*45*
The Scream	*46*
The Fall of Swallows	*47*
The Sailor's Return	*48*
A Wistful Retreat	*49*
Barefoot	*50*

I Departed the Fetid House of My Fathers
 When Even the Fawning Stench Could Not
 Persuade Them to Change Their Name   *51*
Silhouette in Marbled Grey   *52*
Experience Shatters Our Illusions, but Compels Us to
 Forever Collect the Fragments of Their Remains   *53*
A Vain Pursuit   *54*
Voyage of Torment   *55*
Fields of Bone   *56*
Whoever Said Romance Was Dead Did Not
 Understand the Nature of the Cataleptic State   *57*
The Bear Walker   *58*
Leaves   *59*
Perpetual Encore   *60*
Indulgence   *61*
Restricted View   *62*

A COMPLEX ABSOLUTION – THE PROTRACTED GEOMETRY OF FORGIVENESS

It was not so large an area,
The circumference of the circle.
It was only in the drawing of it
That we could not decide
Where the line should be
Permitted to join.

THE FALLOW YIELD

The old man hummed quietly in the cool shade beside a watchtower of sorrow, winding the last burnished yarn of summer onto a skein. In the crowing breeze tambourine leaves turned slowly to autumn, and sated geese flew swollen into a prodigal spread. The old man paused for a moment, rested his song, and briefly read the gnarled journal of his worn hands as a stranger. 'Soon the river will flow too fast, and become too cold to bathe in', thought the old man, as he felt the soft twine slip through his fingers, 'and I will taste nothing but the flavour of winter'. In the mewing distance a crimson veined evening purred, and bedded unfurled claws into the fraying skyline.
As the old man continued to reflect on the passing season, a white mule laden with apples appeared at his side.
The white mule affably extended a cordial salutation, which the old man, although unable to remember any previous encounter with the mule, returned with the warm, easy grace of a fond acquaintance. 'I have often glimpsed you from afar, standing atop the tower, old man,' the mule began, 'and each time have I attempted to understand the purpose of your surveillance.'
The old man would have preferred to remain alone and continue to fix the thread of his broken melody, but he felt awkwardly answerable to the mule's amiable gaze and accordingly scratched his grey bearded chin pensively, allowing himself a

few uncomfortable seconds to form his reply.
'Every day I have climbed this lofty tower and watched. But I am a foolish old man and my vision is dimming. Each sunrise I see less than I did the sunset before, and I watch little but the day receding from my grasp,' he lamented, at once feeling ashamed of his complaint.
'What do you wish to see, old man?' the white mule posed, with a sympathetic smile.
'The expected. Or the unexpected. It makes no difference,' sighed the old man. 'What I wish to see I shall not, and I must settle for any view in its absence.'
Crickets clicked chattering heels, and a peel of cattle bells clanged a languid chorus to accompany the late afternoon's slovenly passage.
'Once I looked out onto a colourful distance which seemed to stretch endlessly into the blue sky, and everywhere I looked I saw myself threshing grain, herding sheep, fishing clear streams. But now I look upon a distance which has caught up with me and I am unable to find myself there.'
'You hoard your sadness as a sleepless old man gathers over-ripe fruit from the tree of dreams, with no thought for the usefulness of his harvest,' the mule advised, shaking it's head softly to and fro.
The old man fell silent for a moment and thought hard on the white mule's words.

'My harvest feeds me well enough. I am an old man and I need nothing more than I can take without reaching.'
'You eat the fruit within your reach, yet the fruit is bitter and you complain of its flavour. How does this satisfy you?'
'I am satisfied by the memory of how it once tasted, even though it has become unpalatable to me now.'
'You have grown fat on your sorrow, old man, perhaps you would care to walk with me for a while, and I will show you a sweeter fruit ripe for the picking.'
The old man thanked the mule gratefully, but made no attempt to stand. 'Perhaps I will find a sweeter fruit of my own soon,' he mused, as he watched the mule retreat.
'Farewell then, old man,' bid the white mule, turning and beginning to walk slowly away. 'I have a long journey ahead, and I must not delay. But I shall remember you well, and I shall think of you often. And I shall see you always in an endless distance, regardless of my station, or whatever view lies before me.'

REPORTING FOR DUTY

The small boy's father dreamed of the sea like
A lover dreams of the scent of skin.
It didn't matter which sea. Any would do:
He needed to escape.
The small boy never dreamed of the sea.
Mostly he dreamed of his father and of
Being a father like him.
One day the small boy watched his father
Wake from a customary short
Summer Sunday afternoon siesta
And soon after, quietly asked:
'What did you dream, father?'
His father looked kindly at the small boy and
Answered unhesitatingly:
'I always dream of you, my son', he purred,
Folding corners of the morning newspaper
Into a sailboat.

VISTA

From here the view extends to nightfall.
Curious ramblers saunter tracing
These worn tracts of hollow earth
Like ancient arms
Weary of stretching for beauty.

APRIL SARABANDE

We two-stepped in the shadow of
The wrecking ball,
Photographing the dance hall with
A confessional eye;
Tossing the timber caber of a
Chance remark
Into the weeping wish that
We had retained
Just one splinter in the palm.

THE COUNT

All gifts of beauty now departed
In sand eyed lamplit bareknuckled bend of day
Childless uncomfortable pillowed on the bell
Losing the count of magpie memories
A familiar stranger unready for the ring.

THE LONG DAY HAS FALLEN

The long day has fallen to the horizon,
A lame nag arrowed in the homeward canter.
The moribund quarry grotesque in its capitulation,
A bloody mount struck riderless into the scar.

(Disingenuous sightseers gawp vulgar at the
Pre-carved spectacle of the withering mundane,
Stand awestruck by their inability to dog ear the page.
Caught between the sentence and the meaning
They punctuate the passage with grunts of ignorance.)

The long day has fallen to the horizon,
Fettered by loss to the stain of disgrace.
Urchins huddle chilled beneath a storm petrel sky
Where a whip crack moonless wind blows their
Seedless husk chalk dust fledgling footprints
Into the Christ hungry dark.

A LINGERING ECLIPSE

A myriad of castles
Occupied the air
Back in those hushed
Evening blueprints of
Impossible constructions.
I'd smoke write clouds
Of delirious rhymes
On damp and
Darkening hills.
You'd picture me in
Chrome studded leather,
Chains of submission,
As we lay adrift in
Separate pastures,
Discovering love and
Thistles in
The meadowsweet.

THE BETROTHAL

Starlight spills a diamond ring
Onto the river banks' finger lustre
Shines back to the unhallowed blue
Like shattered idol filigree fragments
Melded into a questionable mirror.

A CONTINUED POINT OF ARRIVAL

I pulled out of the search party
A motherless child
Bawling to be held.
Tentative waves flailing,
Uncertain stance skewed like a
Graceless hoofer falling
Intoxicated by loss into
The dream splashed brass light
Stained storm porch of morning.
Sheltered from the ogre,
Easy prey for the wolf,
Taunted by the invitation to embrace
A familiar apparition
Reclining on the fresh scented
Soft green turves of yearning,
Necklaced in pearl dew
Where the first mist had risen.

OLD AGE IS A BLOODTHIRSTY BASTARD

Old age is a bloodthirsty bastard,
There's no such thing as a happy ending.
Memories turn on you like a pack of wolves,
Searing your tongue so you can't even lick your wounds.

PHILOSOPHICAL MUSINGS. THE MALE FANTASY DIGNIFIED, AND THE NEGATIVE INFLUENCE OF LOGICAL POSITIVISM ON THE ALREADY PUTATIVE REALITY OF ROMANTIC LOVE

You told me that you loved me,
But not as much as you hated me.
I verified the meaning of the statement:
The sequence checked out. C followed B
Followed A like a dog.
I logically analysed the scientific conclusions.
Collated years of rigorously applying
Empirical experiences (admittedly
This synthetic a posteriori stuff
Can not be proven to exist).
Whispered untested and ultimately
Groundless axioms with tenderness
And unforced affection while you impatiently
Questioned my ability to simultaneously
Occupy two different spaces.
When I laid down my model I
Hoped I could introduce you to exciting
New relationships between physical conditions.
Anticipated jointly evaluating the outcome of
A sampled sequence of random encounters.
Thought we could enjoy observational possibilities.
Alas, my enthusiastic propositions were resoundingly
Confounded by your stark intolerance of my
Continuing compulsion to assiduously
Examine the origins of ethical principles.

CONDITION OF EXISTENCE

We were unable to appreciate
The spectacle of our range:
Daubing ourselves with the
Indelible ochre of doubt, then
Reading each others smears like
Rorschach blots while
Painting wavering lines on
An endless road to meaning.

CHILDHOOD

Childhood is a cemetery of unmarked graves.
Unknown soldiers unarmed,
Cut down in the conflict of
A life lived in moments.

Childhood is the father of the sole survivor,
The bearer of the ruined flag,
The weeper for a fallen army.
The western scud master of the

Slate brume dripping over
Charcoal fields of smouldering summers,
Like a lovesick goose raining
Salty in the crow light.

IN PRAISE OF DESPAIR

You were the wanderer
In my scorched and
Starburned night.
Gathering the lily,
Painting the
Scented notes of
Heartbreak for
The songs of
Imagined angels.

REMEMBRANCE

There are shapes in this sand no tide will fill
Nor any breeze blow nameless into night
And wandering sleepless moments when you
Amble homeward beside me casting no
Glance nor word nor shadow beneath
Broken cinnamon moonshine
Spilling like a thistle in the
Blister of the distance between us.

SYMPHONY

Thunder plays a piano
Piece for left hand
Cello storms after
Woodwind in a
Penguin suit sky
Moonlight intermezzo
Melts into first quiet
Chords of daybreak
Shimmering like
Young leaves on
Branches arced with rain.

**THE SEARCH FOR BEAUTY
IS THE SEED OF PRAYER**

The search for beauty is the seed of prayer
In moon steepled Godless black birth disfigured night
The search for youth is the seed of death
As we scuttle from the fruit like leaves through winter.

NARCOPHOBIA #2 – SHIPWRECKED IN LIMBO

Day calls its lackeys home a red sun
Brands them with the terror of its passing.
Pirate moon shaves sinking sails on a
Spectral skyline awash with mutineer gold.
Chaotically choreographed lifeboat formations occupy
A black lit backstage hinterland slide toward the
Fluctuant coast of sleep, where even
Truth can not hold back bloody buccaneer
Leeched evening pigments oozing
Impenetrable shadows on the restless aisle
Between imagination and belief.

BEACHCOMBERS

They arrive
As though
By accident,
To stroll
Through sands
Of burning yellow.
Finger worn,
Creased at the corners
Of obscure shorelines.
They wade
Joyful in
Comfortable shallow,
Collecting kelp
On bleached toes.
They fall,
Make believe,
Dipping briefly
Beneath the cream
Of broken surf,
To pocket
Tide worn pebbles
And spent shells of
Unforced laughter.

QUESTIONS FOR ALL AGES

We wished our
Fragile voices
Could be
Drowned in song
As we
Patiently waited
For all nine choirs
To break their silence.

THE GREAT STARTING GUN CRIME – ANOTHER SENSELESS STATISTIC

All my life I seem to have
Over exercised caution,
Thought Nigel, jogging around
A catalogue of lame excuses,
And I have continually strained
Every muscle in my body
Through the effort I have spent
On holding myself back.

HARBOUR DAYS
(A Salty Mosaic)

Trawlers brook spent like catches
Beached on sun bleached fenders
Where habitual partners perch dockside
Silent strangers to love. Swallows weave
And children unchecked by possibilities
Bind threads of imagination blind to the
Coarse and half spun fabric of their garb.
Radio incidental counterpoint orchestrates
Conversational preludes. Occasional invitations parade,
While the bayed racket of scavengers circling
Greedy for the spill fills the overmantle grey, where
Old men who can not rig the meter of their jaunt
Chew another windswept cured step toothless
From their Monday morning mile.

SEASONS OF WINTER

These cold days are
The cost of summer,
With the crest of death
Stamped on every kiss
Of waning sunlight.
Swallows return to the
Fumbling hush of our
Wondering bloom,
Beyond the wing of
A crimson sky, wet with
The showering break of
Amaranthine ruins.

AN UNEXPECTED OPPORTUNITY PRESENTS IN THE UNQUIET PITFALLS OF REASON

We were unfocussed in monochrome frames,
Striking the band with the baton of abandon.
Listening for harmonics in a dissonant swell,
While temptation filled our space with numbers
To calculate the dimensions of emptiness.

A RUBY ANNIVERSARY OF THE STAR-CROSSED, COLD CAST, SNAKE-EYED MARRIAGE OF BLOOD AND ASH

Dark shapes
Converge
Menacing silence
Almost
Unseen like
Ghosts
Creeping into
The corners of
Tired eyes.

ANOTHER ONE OF THOSE AWKWARD MOMENTS

It was another one of those
Awkward moments and
Despite my best efforts,
I just couldn't think of
Anything to say.
On any other day I would
Probably have looked
Earnestly sympathetic and
Kept my mouth shut, but
With grieving silence
Ringing out like a peel of
Hammered bronze, I
Felt uncomfortably mute.
Then, right out of nowhere,
I over smiled reassuringly and
Blithely declared to his wife
That the embalmers had
Made him look
The very picture of health.

A GOOD EDUCATION WASTED ON THE PURSUIT OF KNOWLEDGE

From laughter to tears
From smile to smirk
From supplication to song
I have always mistaken
The opening ritual for
The closing ceremony.

LIGHTNING STRIKES THE SAME PLACE TWICE TO SAVE THE STRICKEN FROM MOVING

Stricken feeding loneliness like a hungry dog insatiable
Sour cheese wire smiles. A poor mutt's diet. Unconvincing.
Too frozen moulded desperate to dress the naked vulnerable
                                                         indifferent
Gripped rigid alone in the half lit sneer of a lovers embrace
Like a damned clam clinging to the rock slime of a ruined
                                                          dream
Beneath a pustulated, acned, bastard black night sky.

THE COURTSHIP RITUAL

Now that I am learning
To paint perspective
Everything looks wrong
I set the boat behind the whale
And pitch
A needless harpoon.

THE QUESTION

The small boy wandered into a shady copse of doubt and wrestled with problems he could not resolve. As he knelt down to look more closely at an unusual flower, he suddenly noticed that the flower had disappeared, and in its place he was surprised to see a grey toad. He continued his descent onto the soft ground, and was about to stroke the toad with an outstretched finger, when the toad immediately changed into a young lamb. Amazed and delighted the small boy stroked the young lamb joyfully, ruffling its soft, curly coat until it let out a fearful roar, and at once changed into a bear. The small boy jumped to his feet in terror.
'Don't be afraid,' said the bear.
'But you could harm me!' uttered the small boy nervously.
'I could indeed. And sometimes you will meet me and regret it. But not today.'
'Who are you?' the small boy asked, almost too afraid to move.
'I am truth,' replied the bear, drawing himself up onto his hind legs, looking twice as tall and even more fearsome.
'But you change so quickly and easily,' cried the small boy, awed and shadowed by the bears' huge, upright frame, 'how shall I know it is you if I meet you again?'
'That,' riddled the bear, changing into a cloud and floating away, 'is something that only your own questions will be able to answer.'

A SIMPLE TRANSMUTATION

We never mastered the art of
Speaking bluntly.
Somehow it was always
Easier
To spend endless evenings
Deconstructing simple phrases
To form
Impossibly complicated slogans.

A RESILIENT OPPONENT

Middle age carried
An obvious
Weight advantage,
Shuffled neatly
And put youth on
The deck with a
Stunning right hook.
Gum shield flew out,
The crowd was
On its feet.
Youth beat the count and
Teetered for a moment.
Then grinned back
Defiantly with a
Full set of teeth
Whiter than
Any flag of surrender.

A PERMANENT STATE OF THE TEMPORARY

A permanent state of the temporary furls
Corpulent fish to a pillory of superstition.
Bulled on a diet of industrial effluent they flip
Unable to swim unlabelled between stasis and flux.
Atheists of the unadvertised,
Defenders of the corporate faith,
They puff and blow wheezing
Desperate decks of spoken spells
As if a secret magic will loosen the cuff of an
Interest free credit purchased fear of fresh water.

MASSACRE

We had no comprehension
That our exclamations
Would be put to
A mightier sword.
We were greenhorns, wide eyed
Foot soldiers
Conscripted by artlessness,
Decorated by pride,
Commemorated by
Repercussions of
Bitter and bloody
Conflicts on
Fatuous fields of
Pyrrhic reprisal.

THE SCREAM

'I have arrived at
The end of my ability
To speak without
Repeating myself,'
Cried Martha,
Hollering into a
Canyon of distress,
Refreshing the
Chorus of her echo
Over and over again.

THE FALL OF SWALLOWS

In riveting twilight we polish with softened memories
Quarried moments shelved on
The quiet sighs of
A solemn gathering of years.

In terraplein darkness we glance back briefly
At an empty church
Through lych-gates of dreams
Which have become
Too uncomfortable to sleep on.

THE SAILOR'S RETURN

Like a cast iron anchor bound to the
Grief tangled windlass of my weathered neck
I wore the myrtle wreathed band of a
Sworn pilgrimage to the scent of you
Shining rubied with the bloodshot kiss of a
New moon buried a thousand cuts deep
Beneath the torn heart of spring.

A WISTFUL RETREAT

In the flame marbled morning
We were always young and wise
Gathering tinder for fiery dreams
Painting each day with a new disguise
But starker through the gate of evening
Shirking the staring eye of our sell
A colder sun strokes shadows on our ageing skin
Like a wave of farewell.

BAREFOOT

Sometimes death comes as a marching band
Sometimes hushed as secrets barefoot
Sometimes the cunning cower nervous from the parade
Taken unawares whilst listening for footsteps.

I DEPARTED THE FETID HOUSE OF MY FATHERS WHEN EVEN THE FAWNING STENCH COULD NOT PERSUADE THEM TO CHANGE THEIR NAME

I returned with gifts of anger to the foot of the stoop of your
                                                  indifference
Swept still with the wallowing wind of my repeated descent.
Crushed by a landslide of restlessness, scuttled by the
                                                  realization
That I was always leaving. Forever shelling
Overmannered tributes to the shadowing dead from the
Pockmarked furrow of another nightscarred farewell;
Bruised by the fist of solitude,
Stained by the festering belly of a virgin moon
Falling crippled beneath the open window of its wound.

SILHOUETTE IN MARBLED GREY

You stand before me now,
Barely ticking.
The storm eyed face of a
Cloud painted clock,
Bearded with the
Shade of fallen hours.

EXPERIENCE SHATTERS OUR ILLUSIONS, BUT COMPELS US TO FOREVER COLLECT THE FRAGMENTS OF THEIR REMAINS

In the kindling thirst of solitude
We are tantalized by
Echoes of water.

A VAIN PURSUIT

I thought I could chase you
Further than I could run.
You outpaced me
And left me clutching
The scent of your departure.

VOYAGE OF TORMENT

We circumnavigated a globe of reasons to be
Alighting briefly on islands of doubt.
Serenaded the wounded albatross with
Incantations of repentance and shame,
Clinging buoyed to the essence of each other's song
Like the ghost of Saint Elmo riding shotgun
On the masthead of our cruise.

FIELDS OF BONE

In this field there are scarecrows.
In this field there are no crows.
In this field nothing flies to frighten
With sunken eyes, or spies straw men
Hawk the rattling swag of the bones of
Memories picked fleshless over
The abiding fall of winter.

**WHOEVER SAID ROMANCE WAS DEAD
DID NOT UNDERSTAND THE NATURE
OF THE CATALEPTIC STATE**

Weeping frost spins
Cobwebs onto the hedgerow
Where birdsong tear drops spill
Into the consummated chill of
A gradual dawn.

THE BEAR WALKER

Another birthday stoned me running,
As I stuffed mossy
Cushions of contentment
To break my fall.
Beneath a barnacled sky
I stumbled on logs of uncertainty,
Throwing shadows on solid ground
In a clearing where a
Snake tooth pearly crescent
Cracked moon finger gorged
Raw by insatiable winter,
Beckoned me chilly with a
Sideways grin, like a
Cloud hooded hag,
Into the brewing weald.

LEAVES

Some leaves cling to boney trees
Dead from the fingertips.
Some leaves sing to the
Wind as they sail.
Some leaves offer their beauty to
The pallet of morning.
Some leaves are visibly distressed by
The colour of nightfall.

PERPETUAL ENCORE

Swaddled in the bandied cloth of sleepless prayer,
Cursing the cost of all things holy.
Shying from the flying buttress of apprehension,
Thirsted disconsolate on
Mortgaged lees of a brighter blindness,
Glaring pert through the shallow portal of the glim
As a prematurely grey dawn limps in,
Etched imperfect with the widows hairline
And tenons morning into a marquetry sky
Riddled with harboured songs of grieving.

INDULGENCE

We used to talk about
Everything and nothing.
I'd give you lines like:
'The river of life is swollen by
The souls of the drowned';
You'd wrap your eyes around me
And kiss my soul with the
Fragility of your smile.

RESTRICTED VIEW

This riddled landscape remains
Unquestioned
Unanswered
Your memory
A template of eternity.